Note to Parents and Teachers

The READING ABOUT: STARTERS series introduces key science vocabulary to young children while encouraging them to discover and understand the world around them. The series works as a set of graded readers in three levels.

LEVEL 2: BEGIN TO READ ALONE follows guidelines set out in the National Curriculum for Year 2 in schools. These books can be read alone or as part of guided or group reading. Each book has three sections:

• Information pages that introduce key words. These key words appear in bold for easy recognition on pages where the related science concepts are explained.
• A lively story that recalls this vocabulary and encourages children to use these words when they talk and write.
• A quiz and index ask children to look back and recall what they have read.

Questions for Further Investigation

WHAT'S INSIDE ME? explains key concepts about LIFE PROCESSES. Here are some suggestions for further discussion linked to the questions on the information spreads:

p. 5 *What living things do you see?* Remind children that plants as well as animals are living things, even though they move so slowly it is hard to see their movements.

p. 9 *What bones can you feel under your skin?* You could introduce other names of bones that are easy to find, such as the pelvis, shin bone and elbow (funny) bone.

p. 11 *How can you make your muscles stronger?* Ask children to think about which kinds of exercise work which parts of their body, e.g. swimming, dancing, cycling.

p. 13 *Why do you breathe slower when you are asleep?* Explain how body slows itself down when it sleeps so it can rest. However, brain is still very active, which is why we have dreams, like almost all mammals (so dogs and cats have dreams too)!

p. 15 *When does your heart beat faster?* Ask children to feel their pulse before and after exercise. Could also mention that our heart beats faster when we are excited or scared.

p. 17 *Why do you think your brain is inside your skull?* Your skull protects your brain. Our brain is so important that often we must protect it in other ways, e.g. cycling helmet.

p. 19 *How do senses warn you about danger?* Ask children which senses warn people and animals about different dangers: e.g. fire/hot things, heights, cars, predators etc.

p. 23 *How else can you help your body to feel better?* Ask children to think about what makes them feel good, e.g. having fun, resting, keeping warm/cool in winter/summer.

ADVISORY TEAM

Educational Consultant
Andrea Bright – Science Co-ordinator, Trafalgar Junior School, Twickenham

Literacy Consultant
Jackie Holderness – former Senior Lecturer in Primary Education, Westminster Institute, Oxford Brookes University

Series Consultants
Anne Fussell – Early Years Teacher and University Tutor, Westminster Institute, Oxford Brookes University

David Fussell – C.Chem., FRSC

CONTENTS

© Aladdin Books Ltd 2005

Designed and produced by
Aladdin Books Ltd
2/3 Fitzroy Mews
London W1T 6DF

First published in
Great Britain in 2005 by
Franklin Watts
96 Leonard Street
London EC2A 4XD

A catalogue record for this book is available from the British Library.

ISBN 0 7496 6244 1

Printed in Malaysia

All rights reserved

Editor: Jim Pipe

Design: Flick, Book Design and Graphics

Thanks to:
• The pupils of Trafalgar Infants School, Twickenham for appearing as models in this book.
• Lynne Thompson for helping to organise the photoshoots.
• The pupils and teachers of Trafalgar Junior School, Twickenham and St. Nicholas C.E. Infant School, Wallingford, for testing the sample books.

Photocredits:
l-left, r-right, b-bottom, t-top, c-centre, m-middle
Cover tr, tm & tl, 2ml, 4ml, 11tr, 16c, 31tr — Brand X Pictures. Cover b, 6br, 8mr, 10bl, 12 both, 14 both, 22tl, 23b, 31tr — Marc Arundale/ Select Pictures. 2tl, 3, 4br, 10mr, 11l, 17b, 19br & ml, 21bl, 22tr, 29, 31mr, 31bl, 31br — Comstock. 2bl, 13, 15b, 18 both, 24br, 26br, 31bc — Digital Vision. 5t, 9t, 27mr, 28tr — Eyewire (Photodisc). 5b, 8r, 21tr, 25 all, 28ml, 32 — Ingram Publishing. 6 all (except 6br) — Stockbyte. 7, 17tr — Select Pictures. 9br, 15tr — Jim Pipe. 19tr — PBD. 21t, 22b, 27tl, 30mr — Corbis. 21br, 24tr — Ken Hammond/USDA. 24ml, 26t — Photodisc. 28br — Corel.

READING ABOUT

Starters

LIFE PROCESSES

What's Inside Me?

By Sally Hewitt

Aladdin/Watts
London • Sydney

Plants and **animals** are **alive**.
You are a kind of **animal** so you are **alive**.

Plants and **animals** are **living** things.
All **living** things do the same things.

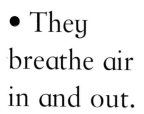

• They need
food and water.

• They move.

• They
breathe air
in and out.

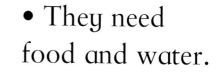

4

• **Living** things can sense the world around them.

• They grow and they make new life like themselves.

• Look around you. What living things can you see?

Food gives you **energy**. Different **foods** help to keep you strong and healthy.

**Eggs,
nuts,
meat**

**Brown bread,
pasta**

**Cheese,
milk**

**Vegetables,
fruit**

Eat some of these different kinds of **food** every day. Your body needs lots of water every day, too!

6

You chew your **food**. You swallow it.
The **food** goes into your **stomach**.
Your **stomach** mashes
it up.

Your blood carries
goodness from the
food all around
your body.

Stomach

You get
rid of waste
that you don't
need when you
go to the toilet.

• Follow food with your finger on its journey through
the boy's body. Then imagine it inside your body.

Your **bones** make a frame for your body called a **skeleton**.

Your **skeleton** protects the soft parts inside your body.

Without a **skeleton** your body would have no shape!

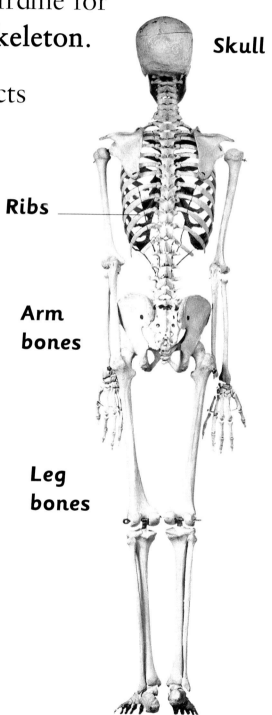

Skull

Ribs

Arm bones

Leg bones

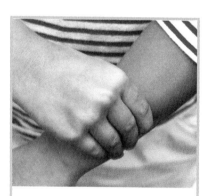

You can feel strong bones under your skin.

8

Your arms and legs bend at your elbows and knees.

Elbows and knees are called **joints** because they are where your **bones join** together.

Your wrists, ankles and neck are **joints**, too.

• What bones can you feel under your skin?

You can **move** because you have **muscles** all over your body.

You have small **muscles** in your face. Feel them pull your skin when you smile.

You have big **muscles** in your back, legs and arms.

Big muscles pull your bones when you move.

Face muscles

Your **muscles** work hard when you run and jump.

Exercise keeps **muscles** strong and healthy.

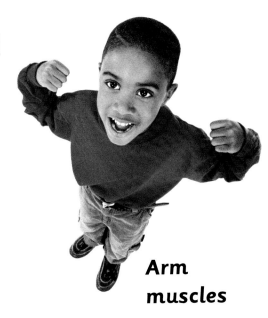

Arm muscles

Stand on tiptoe. Feel the **muscle** in the back of your leg bulge.

Dancers have strong **muscles** in their legs.

• How can you make your muscles stronger?

Behind your ribs are your two **lungs**.
You **breathe** air with your **lungs**
all day and all night.

**Feeling
your lungs**

Feel your **lungs** fill with
fresh air as you **breathe**
in. Feel them empty as
you **breathe** out.

Stale air from
your lungs fills
a balloon when
you blow it up.

12

You need **oxygen** from the air to stay alive. So you must **breathe** all the time.

When you exercise, your body needs more **oxygen**.
Your lungs must work hard.

After exercise you **breathe** in and out very fast.

Exercise

• Why do you breathe slower when you are asleep?

Your **heart** is also behind your ribs. It is a strong muscle that **pumps blood** all around your body.

You can hear your **heart pumping** in your chest. This is called your heartbeat.

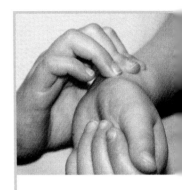

Feel your pulse beat in your wrist. It's your heartbeat!

Listening to heart

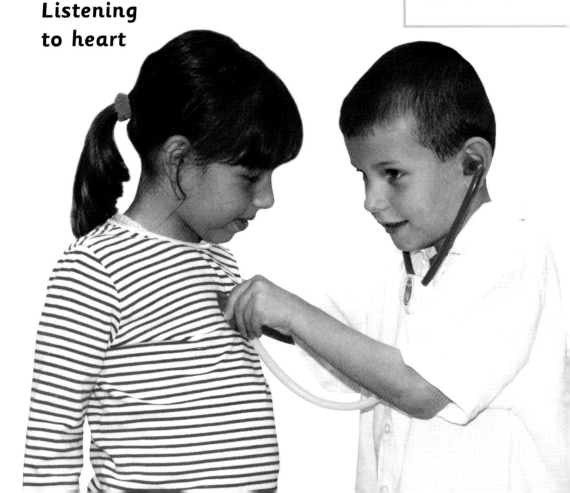

Blood flows around your body through tubes called **blood vessels**.

When you have a cut, you see your **blood**. The **blood** dries into a scab. Your skin gets better below it.

Cut

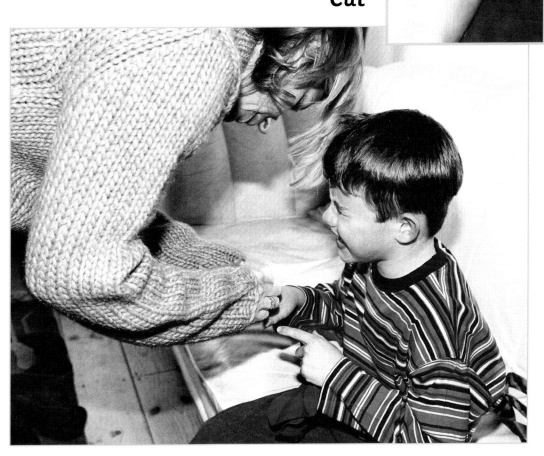

• When does your heart beat faster?

You have a **brain** that controls everything you do.

All animals have **brains**. But only humans can talk, read and write.

You **think** with your **brain**.

It is more powerful than any computer.

Computer

16

Your **brain** is in your head. It sends messages to the rest of your body.

Your **brain** tells the rest of your body what to do.

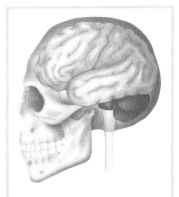

Your brain is soft, like a grey, wrinkly sponge.

• Why do you think your brain is inside your skull?

Your **senses** tell you what
is going on around you.

You taste with your tongue
and smell with your nose.

You see with your eyes
and hear with your ears.
You feel with your skin.

Your **senses** also warn you about danger!

Your eyes, ears, nose, tongue and skin are connected to your brain.

They send messages back to your brain. Your brain tells you what you are **sensing**.

Your senses keep you safe. You look and listen for traffic before you cross the road.

Seeing a dog

• How do your senses warn you about danger?

A human **baby grows** inside its mother.
After nine months it is ready to be born.

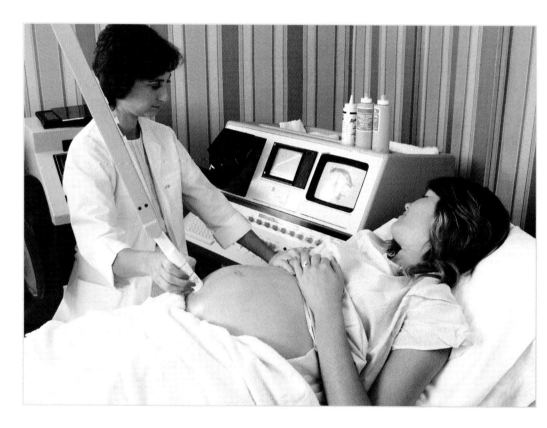

A **baby** drinks its mother's milk.

It needs to be looked after all the time.

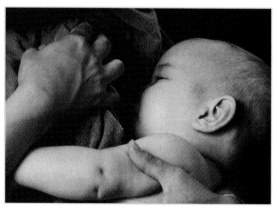

20

Baby

A **baby grows** into a child.
A child **grows** into a teenager.
A teenager **grows** into
an adult.

When you
become an
adult you will
stop **growing**.

But you won't
stop changing
and learning
new things!

• What clues tell you how old someone is?

Tiny germs can give you a cold. Use a hanky if you sneeze so no one else catches the germs.

When you feel **ill**, you go to the doctor. The doctor takes your temperature and feels your pulse.

You may need **medicine** to help you get better.

If you need an operation, you may go to hospital.

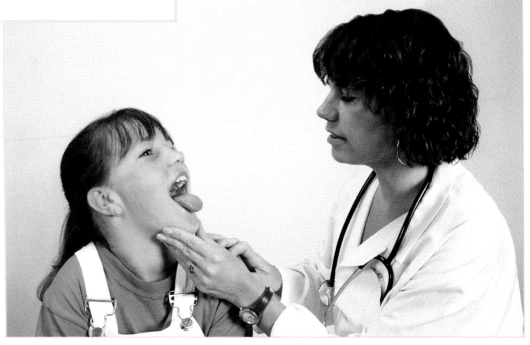

You can help yourself stay **healthy**.

You can eat good food, drink lots of water and get plenty of exercise and sleep.

• How else can you help your body to *feel better*?

A DAY AT THE BEACH

Look out for words about your **body**.

Poppy and Adam were very excited. They were going to the beach.

"Are you too old to come too, Grandad?" asked Adam.

Grandad laughed. "My **bones** are a bit creaky. The sea will do them good!" he said.

"Can **baby** Jake swim with us?" asked Poppy.

"Not until he **grows** a bit," said Mum.

"But he'll love the soft sand."

24

"I'll make the picnic,"
said Mum.
"We'll need lots of **food**
and plenty of drinks."

"I can't find my swimsuit!" said Adam.
"**Think** hard," said Mum. "I remember!"
said Adam. "It's in my sports bag."

"I'll get the buckets
and spades,"
said Poppy.

"Don't forget hats
and sun cream to protect
your skin," said Dad. "And sunglasses, too!"

When they got there, the sun was shining.

"The sea makes you feel **alive!**" said Grandad.
"I can feel the sand in my toes!" said Mum.
"I can taste the salty sea air!" said Poppy.
"I can hear the waves!" said Dad.

"I'll take a picture,"
said Grandad.

"Smile everyone!"

"Let's go for a swim," said Dad.

"Look, your friends are already in the water."

"Can we blow up my ring?" asked Poppy.
"Yes," said Dad, "But you'll need strong **lungs**."

"Watch me swim underwater!" said Adam. "But you can't **breathe** underwater!" said Poppy. "I'll hold my **breath**," said Adam.

Adam and Dad went for a swim. Poppy played with her ring in the shallow water.

When they arrived they were out of **breath**. Poppy could feel her **heart pumping** fast.

"Where's our sandcastle?" asked Poppy. "Did it **move**?"

"Look!" said Adam. "The tide came in. We're standing on it!"

"Let's use our **brains** next time and build one further from the sea!" laughed Poppy.

Think about an activity you enjoy, such as going swimming. Can you write a list of the parts of your body you might use? Or draw pictures to show how your body works.

If I cut myself, the blood will dry into a scab.

I have big muscles in my arms. I can swing on the bars.

QUIZ

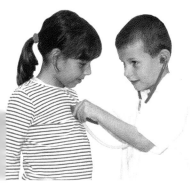

How can you keep your
muscles strong and healthy?

Answer on page 11

What does
your **heart** do?

Answer on page 14

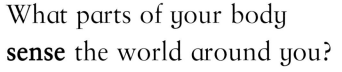

What parts of your body
sense the world around you?

Answer on page 18-19

Children are living things.
What are these children doing?
What else can living things do?

Have you read this book? Well done! Do you remember these words? Look back and find out.

INDEX